C000174655

THE
MEETING
BOOK

MEETINGS THAT ACHIEVE AND DELIVER – EVERY TIME

Published by
LID Publishing Ltd
One Adam Street
London
WC2N 6LE
United Kingdom

31 West 34th Street, Suite 8004,
New York, NY 1001, US

info@lidpublishing.com
www.lidpublishing.com

A member of:

BPR

Business Publishers Roundtable

www.businesspublishersroundtable.com

Printed in the Czech Republic by Finidr

ISBN: 978-1-910649-74-9

Cover and page design: Caroline Li
Illustration: Tom Russell, Inky Thinking

THE
MEETING
BOOK

MEETINGS THAT ACHIEVE AND DELIVER – EVERY TIME

HELEN CHAPMAN

LONDON · NEW YORK · BOGOTA
MADRID · BARCELONA · BUENOS AIRES
MEXICO CITY · MONTERREY · SAN FRANCISCO
SHANGHAI

CONTENTS

DEDICATION

For my beautiful children,
Ellie, Peter and Ruby.

Feel proud about who you are
and always trust your cape.

THANK YOU

To Luke Varda for bringing inspiration and new horizons.

To my family who love and support me whether I write a book or make a cake.

To the people who helped me learn. Among them Leigh Collis with whom it all began, Jerry Hogeveen who taught me group process, Paul Levesque who encouraged a glimmer of talent, Ruud Janssen Veneboor for that 'Tamagotchi moment', Jane Myers Lewis for real conversations, Robert Putnam for great coaching and Nikki, Sara and the LID team for championing this book.

To my precious clients for everything we create together.

To the fantastic TFP Facilitators and Inky Thinkers who make meetings extraordinary.

And, most importantly, to Tom Russell, Catherine Hennessy and Ben Robinson for their courage, wisdom, humour and friendship, all of which made this book possible.

INTRODUCTION

Are you on your way to a meeting?

Have you prepared? Do you expect it to go well? Are you stepping into a waste of time? Are you preparing yourself for conflict? Whatever frame you hold about that meeting - you will probably be right.

It is tempting to blame others for poor meetings, but, whatever your role, it's your job to make sure that meeting is a success.

I have written this book to help you bring about lasting, positive change for every meeting you are involved with.

In these pages are observations and reasoning to help you:
- Sharpen your perspective on meetings.
- See through a new meeting lens.
- Be more intentional about meeting purpose.
- Understand your own responsibility and impact in meetings alongside others.
- Be smart about the way you put meetings together.
- Make choices about information sharing.

This book is a meeting of minds: mine and yours.

I offer insight and provocation and you apply your own wisdom to make choices about the adjustments you need to make.

How good can we make it?

This book is not a paint-by-numbers approach to writing agendas.
We can do better than that.

This section will begin to open up thinking.

I ❤ MEETINGS
LET'S DISCUSS

OPEN TO
A FRESH
PERSPECTIVE

THE DAY I REALIZED

1996: LONDON: A HOT WEDNESDAY AFTERNOON IN MID-SEPTEMBER

I'm in a meeting. The table is long and rectangular with 14 other people seated around it. I'm representing my business and brand alongside a number of people representing theirs. There exists an invisible, yet palpable, hierarchy and pecking order that is linked to the size and success of each brand. These people are like gods and archangels to me.

I'm usually bright and enthusiastic and a good communicator, but when I sit around this table (which I do every six weeks or so) – I seem to lose my power of speech and feel intimidated by the others. It might be something to do with the weak smiles I seem to receive when I speak, or it might all be in my mind. I don't know. Every time I come here I tell myself "this time I'll contribute more", then without fail, just like today, I can't seem to get my words out. It all feels so formal to me; so stiff, so awkward – I have to do something to lighten the mood (or risk insanity).

During the first break, I take out my four-year-old daughter's Tamagotchi (her digital pet I'd promised to keep alive while she was at nursery). The consultant leading the meeting notices and asks what I am doing – I tell him and he laughs out loud. A new conversation begins around the group. The atmosphere is lighter. People share stories about their digital pets (!) which leads to smiles. The ice is broken. We have something in common. The meeting moves on. It is much more relaxed now. Wow! Who knew? Something so simple... and after all that stress too!

This one small memory is laced with rich information, and I remember being there very clearly.

What meeting story would you tell me in return?

On that day, 20 years ago, I knew something had to give. That one simple move shifted the whole atmosphere in the group, not just for that meeting but for my future meetings. It got me thinking about the other moves I could make in meetings to make them better for me and for everyone else present. That's what aroused my curiosity.

2016: LONDON: A RAINY SUNDAY MORNING IN EARLY MAY

These days I jump out of bed to facilitate meetings. I help groups make the complex simple to work with. It's the most glorious job in the world. In fact, it isn't work.

A NEW WAY OF SEEING

THE MEETING KALEIDOSCOPE™

No matter how experienced you are in meetings, I know you face different groups of challenges on a regular basis. The room is filled with a curious mix of sights, sounds, noises and feelings. The Meeting Kaleidoscope™ reflects the dynamic and shifting nature of working with people, in real time.

Take a look at the genius that is the kaleidoscope. It is an optical instrument with small pieces of coloured glass contained at the end of a tube. At the end of the tube are usually three rectangular mirrors set at 60° to one another so that they form an equilateral triangle.

When the tube is rotated, the viewer can see the continually changing symmetrical forms created by the coloured glass reflected in two or more of the mirrors. With each rotation, the tumbling of the glass creates varying colours and patterns. The patterns are revealed as a beautiful, symmetrical colour is created by the reflections; a multiple and constant reflection of colour. All it takes is a small twist at the end of the kaleidoscope to adjust and change the pattern. The viewer decides when to twist it and whether to make small or large twists.

The Meeting Kaleidoscope is a model developed to make the complex simple to work with by separating out each component part of a meeting so that it may be sharpened, refined and made fit for purpose.

The model operates in the same way as a real kaleidoscope – only, this time, instead of coloured glass, this magical tube comprises the four component parts that exist in every meeting:

- **The purpose of the meeting**
- **The people in the meeting**
- **The process of the meeting**
- **The content being shared**

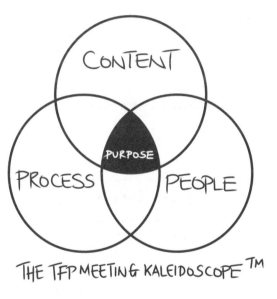

THE TFP MEETING KALEIDOSCOPE ™

The Meeting Kaleidoscope consists of a lens that is used to separate, see and understand the barrage of sensory information present before, during and after meetings. Being able to see which part of the kaleidoscope is showing up strongest will give you focused insight into what's going on; for example, too much or too little content, process flows and blocks, levels of emotion and engagement.

By using this model you are able to make conscious decisions to see what is happening in a meeting. You can then attend to the quality of a meeting by making twists (or choices) that will increase or decrease the size of each component. This will help to achieve a 'sweet spot' where all components coincide harmoniously to create a meeting that achieves and delivers every time.

So you might find the Meeting Kaleidoscope a helpful tool if you find that your meetings:

- Lack purpose and focus.
- Are so content-heavy that they become cumbersome and unwieldy.
- Include participants who contribute little.
- Are poorly attended.
- Rarely reach shared decisions that make things happen outside the meeting.

Twisting the Meeting Kaleidoscope to focus on each element can be done before, during or after a meeting. It can also be used for meetings with varying numbers of participants, from one-to-one meetings or small team meetings, to meetings of groups of 100 or more. These elements interact with one another to create patterns of understanding and experience. Whether you are the meeting owner, participant, expert, chair, facilitator (or anything else), you can use this model to work and self-supervise, in a simple, yet cognitive, way.

Spotting what is going on in a meeting through this lens helps you to make adjustments (twist the kaleidoscope) to find the sweet spot where all of the components come together in service of the group and the meeting result.

With each twist made, you will see what is (or is not) required, depending on whether any one component is lacking or dominating. That means that, in any given moment, you can be clear about various aspects of the meeting, including:

- Where you are at any moment during a meeting; for example, just getting started or at a decision-making point.
- The conditions for success – which may require the sizing up or down of each part of the kaleidoscope; for example, heavy information sharing may need to be digested with a good process.
- The central sweet spot of purpose where the combination of all four components coincide optimally to create clear focus.
- The adjustments you need to make, why and how; for example, more or less information, the choice of discussion process, right people, right focus.
- The behaviour you need to bring to the meeting: how you show up; where your attention is; your intention.
- The beliefs you hold and the choices about how you engage
- Your personal responsibility before, during and after the meeting, regardless of your role.

Purpose, people, process and content are the four big areas on which to focus, if you are serious about having meetings that achieve and deliver every time.

By exploring all four in detail you will discover where you can improve every meeting. The most sensible place to begin is with purpose....

"Start with WHY"
Simon Sinek, author, speaker, and consultant

Let's get To The Reality Of Your Meetings Today....
This section will help you to take a good look at the purpose and
context of your meetings.

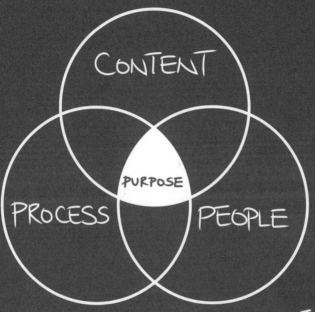

PART TWO

THE TFP MEETING KALEIDOSCOPE ™

TWIST 1

PURPOSE

SEVEN VIEW POINTS

LOOK AT A MEETING FROM ALL SIDES

Definition 1
Meeting [*noun*]
"When two or more people come together to share, discuss, create, decide."

Definition 2
To meet [*verb*]
"To face or eye, directly or without avoidance."
"To join at an agreed or designated place or time."

The Holy Grail:
Meetings should be agile and maximize the potential of the people and resources available.

Do yours?

Flexibility:
Meetings can be fast, long, virtual, formal, informal, face-to-face, large or small.

How flexible are your meetings? Are yours stuck in a routine?

Culture:
Meetings can add to, or detract from, a business performance culture.

Done well, they add vibrancy, colour, rigour and intentionality. Done poorly, they bring grey 'hum-drum' and slow things down.

Do your meetings add to the performance of the business? Really?

Risk:
Meetings can fragment and block an organization. Done well, they oil the rhythm and flow of an organization; done poorly they hinder things and divert attention away from what really matters.

Do your meetings carry any risks for your organization?

Opportunity:
When carried out with the organization's goals and rhythms in mind, meetings can unlock resource, synchronize and liberate the organization.

What is important for you and your organization here?

What is already becoming clear about the PURPOSE of your meetings?

THE PUSH AND PULL OF YOUR MEETINGS

ARE YOU IN CONTROL?

Are you reading this between meetings?

When do you find time to do the work?

What are you in control of?

Think about your typical work day. How many hours a week do you spend:

- Attending meetings?
- Preparing for meetings?
- Following up after meetings?
- In meeting rooms, or at your desk, or while you're driving?
- In 'chance' meetings at the coffee machine?

You get the picture. Your day is probably filled with speaking to people, or needing to speak to people about important things. The chances are that you will get around to speaking to them, but you have so many meetings it feels like a battle to fit everything in.

Meetings that deliver and achieve every time begin with you making good choices about which meetings to call and which meetings to attend.

I bet you face a mixed picture when it comes to meetings – some go well and some not so well; some are worthwhile and some are not. Or perhaps they're all a bit so-so.

They may be slowing you down; making you feel busy and (maybe) also making you feel important?

Do you ever say "no" to a meeting, conference call, conference, project? If you do, is it because you literally cannot squeeze it in – because you're too busy with other meetings literally back-to-back? Or do you say "no" for other reasons?

It is worth remembering that no matter whether you attend, chair or facilitate a meeting, to give it your best attention, your personal purpose must be clear. If you are focused and purposeful about how you dedicate your time, there's a good chance your meetings will be more purposeful too. It's time to start making conscious choices and taking back control.

It's time to sharpen the focus and clarity of why. Why this meeting? Why now? Why you? To achieve this clarity, you have to make a conscious choice. You have more control of that.

EVOLUTION

COMMUNICATION AND ADAPTATION

There are two big reasons why human beings are among the most successful species on Earth: we have learned to communicate and to adapt. These two strengths alone have (so far) secured our place in the world – that's compelling and truly amazing.

Granted, as a species, we don't all see eye-to-eye. Granted, there are pushers and pullers. Granted, the voices of the few seem louder than the voices of the many. Granted, we don't always treat each other, or our precious world, as well as we could.

BUT we are here. We are in this together, with our ancestry reaching back about six million years, with the modern form of humans only evolving about 200,000 years ago; although civilization as we know it is only about 6,000 years old.

We've survived:

The Old Stone Age
The New Stone Age
The Bronze Age
The Iron Age
The Middle Ages

And now we are here... in the Modern Age.

While communication and adaptation have been our prevailing strengths, they still have not reached full potential in this modern world. We continue to fall into traps that knock our human interaction off track.

Yet, when a clear purpose combines with a true willingness to communicate and adapt, meetings become vibrant, engaging, valuable... and enjoyable.

Meetings have helped guide us through generations – through revolutions and wars, with world leaders and communities. In many eras of our existence, people meeting with each other provided the glue that kept communities strong and focused; sometimes from sheer necessity of saving lives, and sometimes for the sheer joy of being with like-minded people.

With our vibrant history in mind, it is disappointing to see that in business, meetings have become lacklustre and in many places 'the grey meeting routine' prevails. In these places meetings are habitual and routine, and serve very little purpose. Unlike great wisdoms that are handed down through generations with care, meetings have been passed down through the years like a game of 'meetings Chinese whispers' where all sense and reason have become lost.

Despite this, meetings are very much alive today. They are alive with human beings. Teams; groups; co-workers; managers; sports teams; boy scouts; parish councils; local councils. Meetings take place in scout huts; church halls; hotels; purpose-built meeting spaces; they happen face-to-face; by phone; online; via webcam.

Whether it's a few people meeting over coffee or 100 people in a conference room, meetings happen all the time. Everywhere.

Perhaps the thought of adapting your meetings feels overwhelming? After all, there are a lot of them and there is only one of you.

How can you do that?

Your first step is simple and powerful. It all begins in your mind: twist the Meeting Kaleidoscope such that you:

- **Decide to put a conscious focus on your meetings.**
- **Decide to adapt your meetings.**
- **Decide to communicate well in them.**
- **Decide to make them intentional and purposeful.**

You may not fully understand how yet, but your conscious decisions will unlock new awareness and new possibilities.

A belief I hold is summed up well in this quote by the author James Redfield:

"Where attention goes energy flows; where intention goes energy flows!"

STOP GOING
TO MEETINGS

THE WHAT AND WHY OF YOUR PRIORITIES

One leader recently told me that he asked people in his organization to stop being in meetings. He said the crunch came when he discovered that a customer had found it quicker to contact a competitor to place an important order than to contact his team, because – guess what – his team were unavailable to speak to the customer because they were in meetings. The customer grew frustrated about being put on hold and made to wait, so he went elsewhere.

Ironic isn't it? Customers are left holding on the line while the organization has meetings about how to delight 'the customer'.

Meetings about important things become self-perpetuating, vicious circles. Meetings are called to discuss priorities. They are called to make plans about the priorities. They are called to change the priorities and then to adjust the plans.

Organizations continually cycle through continuous and progressive priorities. The cycle typically involves being externally focused on the customer, then looping back around to being internally process focused (no doubt to fix an internal process because of some customer feedback), before looping back to being externally focused again. And so it goes on. External focus and internal focus – on and on.

(This, by the way, is why many change programmes happen).

Everything becomes a priority. Then priorities overlap with other priorities and before you know it, you're needed on every project team (and if you're not, you wonder why not). Without realizing, in a blink, you're 'back-to-back' with projects and meetings. It's exhausting just thinking about it.

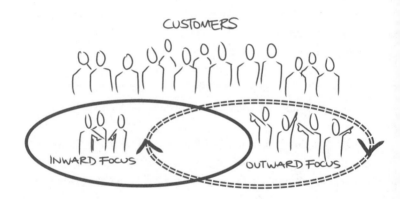

That leader I mentioned made a conscious, intentional, decision to adapt. He didn't want the people in his organization to stop going to meetings per se, instead, his request was for each person to choose to have the right conversation at the right time with the right people about the right things, to make his organization work. If those conversations must take place in a meeting, then so be it, but they must be efficient, purposeful and decisive.

Perhaps it's time for you to stop 'going to meetings' and instead, ask yourself:

- **Which conversations do I need to have?**
- **With whom?**
- **What is important about those conversations?**
- **What do I need from them and how does that serve my work?**
- **Do I have to be 'in a meeting' to achieve that?**

These questions are a great alternative to always preparing for, rushing to and slogging through, meeting after meeting. Step off that hamster wheel. Decide to change the collective story.

Stop writing time lists and calling them agendas.
Stop the routine meetings for the sake of meetings.
Stop wasting time – yours and others – in meetings that are unnecessary.
Stop wasting money – add up the cost of all those hours sitting in meeting rooms (it amounts to a small fortune).
The blah ....the hot air and the aimless noise.

Imagine yourself saying:

"Our meetings oil the wheels of our organization – they serve our progress no matter what cycle we're in."

"Our meetings are where decisions are made and people are clear about their contributions."

"Our meetings are agile enough to get the job done quickly and accurately."

"Our meetings are thorough enough to create depth and understanding so that people are aligned and the right things happen."

Begin to prioritize now; ask yourself these questions:

WHAT REALLY NEEDS MY ATTENTION NOW? HOW DO I KNOW?

WHAT NEEDS ME TO BE INVOLVED SUCH THAT IF I WASN'T SOMETHING WOULD BE LOST OR MISSING?

WHAT MEETINGS AM I INVOLVED WITH AND WHY?

WHAT NEW BEHAVIOUR CAN I BEGIN NOW THAT COULD TRANSFORM MY MEETINGS AND HOW I ENGAGE WITH OTHERS?

What meetings am I involved with? Why?

_____

_____

_____

What really needs my attention now? How do I know?

_____

_____

_____

What needs my involvement to the point that if I wasn't there, something would be lost or missing?

_____

_____

_____

What new behaviour can I begin now that could transform my meetings and how I engage with others?

_____

_____

_____

START HAVING THE RIGHT CONVERSATIONS

CONNECT MEETING PURPOSE WITH YOUR ORGANIZATION'S PURPOSE

Think about your organization.

What is the compelling **purpose** of your organization? Can you say it in one simple sentence that would make me stop in my tracks and want to know more?

Next, think about the **'big goals'** that enable that purpose – what are they? Can you describe them simply and clearly for anyone to understand?

What about the **people** in your organization or team: what do they know, what are they capable of that achieves the goals to enable the purpose?

Next, think about maximizing their collective wisdom and power so that there is a straight and direct line between their energy and focus and the goals and purpose of your organization.

Anything that's not on that straight and direct line, anything that pulls them or you off-track is probably the 'busy, busy' and not adding direct value.

Start to choose consciously the <u>meetings you call</u>, to serve what I have just described.

Start to choose consciously the <u>meetings you attend</u>, to serve what I have just described.

Meetings that achieve and deliver are the ones that unlock the potential of people to make the right things happen for your organization.

The meeting culture in your organization must be:

    1. Agile enough to get the job done quickly and accurately.

    2. Thorough enough to create depth and understanding.

This applies to each and every meeting. Whether they are shift hand-over meetings, project team meetings, strategy creation meetings, problem-solving meetings or conferences, make every conversation serve the group and power your organization.

So, break it down by thinking clearly about your organization.

WHAT'S IT'S **BIG** PURPOSE?

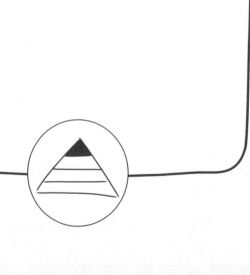

WHAT ARE YOUR ORGANIZATION'S
BIG GOALS THAT ARE DESIGNED TO
SERVE THE BIG PURPOSE?

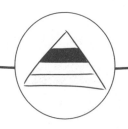

HOW ALIGNED ARE YOUR **PEOPLE & MEETINGS** TO THE BIG GOAL & THE BIG PURPOSE

Now think about your meetings.

Can you draw a direct line that connects the meetings you call and attend to the overall purpose of your organization?

For every meeting ask yourself:

- Why does that meeting need to happen at all?
- Why does it need to happen now?
- Why do you really need to be there?

If you can't give a clear answer – why are you having the meeting?

A CALL TO THE IMAGINATION

HOW GOOD CAN IT GET?

"Vision is seeing what life could be like while dealing with life as it is"
Richard Olivier, Inspirational Leadership

Take a look at how your 'meeting life' is now, and compare that with how it could be.

Look at that word 'meeting'.

- What do you think?
- What memories pop up?
- What images spring to mind?
- How does it make you feel?

Now, imagine the best-ever meeting, a world-class meeting

- What do you think?
- What would make it the best ever?
- What images spring to mind?
- How does it make you feel?

How close is your reality to your vision of a perfect meeting? Perhaps you've just spotted the gap. Whether it is a small or large gap, your meetings can be better.

Use this process to help think this through (feel free to do this in words or in pictures – whatever suits you best).

- Describe the ideal meeting you would like to create; be as free with your imagination as you dare.

_____

_____

_____

- Describe the current meeting situation; be as specific as you can about today's reality.

_____

_____

_____

- Highlight the gap between both pictures, and underline the things that need tuning up.

_____

_____

_____

Find the ways to move towards the new picture while dealing with life as it is.

- What will it take to get you to switch from the same old meetings?
- What is the pain of sticking with the same?
- What is the pleasure of becoming more resourceful?

Adapt to the new. How do you do that? You have to create the path. You have to do the work.

NOW, GO AHEAD, CALL TO YOUR 'IMAGINATION'

By the way, if you're the person who says "I've got a rubbish imagination", the fact that you're even thinking that is evidence that your imagination exists.

Human Beings : Being Humans

"Man evolved to feel strongly about few people, short distances, and relatively brief intervals of time, and these are still the dimensions of life that are important"
Malcolm Gladwell, journalist and author

The sole focus of this section is to consider the most resourceful, capable and creative of all; people
– without whom meetings would not be possible.

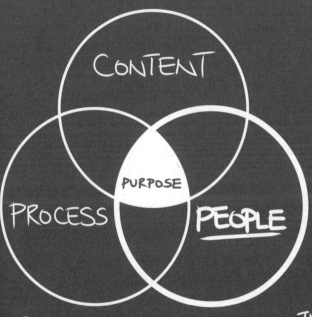

PART THREE

THE TFP MEETING KALEIDOSCOPE ™

TWIST 2

PEOPLE

YOU

*"The single most powerful asset we all have is our mind.
If it is trained well, it can create enormous wealth in what seems
to be an instant"*

Robert T Kiyosaki, *Rich Dad, Poor Dad*

It can be tempting to look at others in a meeting and think of them as the reason you cannot get your point across, or don't get enough airspace, or why decisions don't get made.

You already know that yours is the only behaviour you can influence.

Is there a meeting version of you?
How would you describe the meeting version of you?

Do you adjust the meeting version of yourself depending on the people in front of you?

Why is that?

Consider the following to create a better, more resourceful meeting version of you:

- **Balance awareness of yourself with a keen and curious awareness of others.**
- **Offer opinion along with facts and be able to distinguish between the two.**
- **Contribute your ideas and thinking to serve the conversation rather than to serve yourself.**
- **Ask questions based on a genuine interest to hear what others think.**
- **Listen to others as if your life depends on it so that your thinking benefits from the thoughts of others.**
- **Know that to understand is your top priority. Suspend making a judgment of agreement or disagreement until you have fully understood the thoughts being shared.**

MEETINGS ARE A COLLECTION OF WANDERING, UNRULY MINDS

"People are fun to notice –
Their eyes taking off like birds
Away from their words...."

Elma Mitchell, *People Etcetera*

Every meeting, no matter how large or small, is dependent on the dynamic interaction of human minds. Yet, I believe that the human mind is wandering and unruly. It wanders, it gets side-tracked, it gets bored, it gets frustrated, it gallops ahead. It is not at its best when it's boxed in.

Why wandering and unruly? Well, imagine a typical meeting scene and then speed up the sequence. You'll be likely to:

- See people talking at (rather than to or with) one another.
- Hear the hum of "blah blah blah".
- See expressions ranging from eyes half-closed to eyes diverted towards laptops, phones, or windows.
- Feel the vibration of knee jiggling and finger tapping.
- See folded arms and slumped shoulders.
- Notice a noise that is ever-present (sometimes there's even noisy silence – the noise of people diverting or withdrawing their attention).
- See people buttoning their lips and sucking their teeth.

Now, add to this scene a rigid meeting agenda. It's no wonder people grow fidgety. They have way more to offer and yet they have to endure a forced sequence that may or may not have real meaning.

Why try to harness human minds with a tight, controlled, rigorous agenda? Would your own impatient, wandering mind be harnessed by being forced into submission with an endless agenda? I believe you are missing a big opportunity if you try to control those human minds with a strict agenda. Why would you want to?

You have to be smarter than that.

Instead, you could decide to work with unruliness and wandering rather than battling to contain it. Embracing and encouraging them will take a big step closer to having meetings that achieve and deliver every time.

So what should you do?

First: accept that meetings are alive, they are constantly changing, *living* patterns.

Second: **consciously twist the Meeting Kaleidoscope to:**

1. **Focus meeting conversations on the purpose of the meeting.**
2. **Make sure that every individual knows why they are needed in this meeting; and why now?**
3. **Practice focus rather than restraint or control.**
4. **Ditch any agenda item that does not contribute to that purpose (less, done well, is most definitely best).**
5. **Engage the minds of participants with a process that stretches thinking rather than squashing it.**

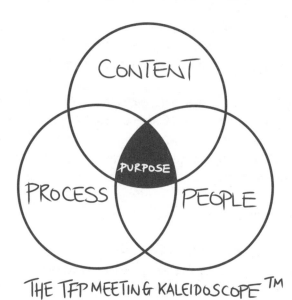

THE TFP MEETING KALEIDOSCOPE ™

ACCEPT THAT WE'RE IN THIS TOGETHER

*"It is well to remember that the entire universe,
with one trifling exception, is composed of others"*

John Holmes, poet

On the subject of people, take a good look at the people around you. You need them and they need you. Together, it is possible to have meetings that achieve and deliver every time.

Recognize that it is not compulsory to feel warm and fluffy around everyone in your meetings. The basic ingredients for a good meeting relationship is mutual respect and a shared purpose.

Accept that there will be times when you 'bump into others' with your views, opinions, values and behaviour. There is nothing wrong with having different views and opinions; in fact, those differences of opinion should be encouraged and treasured because that is where new possibilities lie.

I've noticed a growing tendency for people, after just one lively exchange, to jump to a premature conclusion such as "oh, we'll never agree" or "we don't see eye-to-eye". They then work hard to prove this assumption is true, meeting after meeting, until positions become so entrenched that conflict becomes a reality.

Whatever happened to a frank and healthy exchange of opinion and knowledge that serves to broaden perspective and increase options?

Avoid this trap by accepting that you're in meetings with 'others' and hold this frame of mind to help yourself maintain perspective. Your view is one of many. Your view will contribute to the thinking as a whole. Your view 'just is'. It is neither right nor wrong. It is simply your view. Offer it to others with the intention of helping them to understand your perspective. Invite others to share their perspectives and open your mind to the developing conversation.

This approach is in stark contrast to the alternative (and more usual) approach in meetings where people give their opinion and then defend it, come what may. That has little to do with exploring thinking and more to do with enjoying winning an argument or debate. It may feel good that you are able to convince and persuade others in the moment, but in the end, that will not grow real understanding nor lead to reaching a decision that everybody supports.

I work with these four beliefs, they may help you too:

- **People work perfectly:** no-one is wrong or broken – including yourself.
- **People act sensibly in their own minds.**
- **Underneath every behaviour is a positive intention:** that is, to achieve something of benefit.
- **People respond to their experience, not to reality itself:** our senses, beliefs and past experience give us a map of the world from which we operate; in other words, we create our own reality.

These are 4 of 13 central principles of neuro-linguistic programming (NLP), an approach to communication, personal development,
and psychotherapy created by Richard Bandler and John Grinder in
the 1970s

Like you, other people are probably rushing from one meeting to
the next, following up after a meeting, or preparing for the next one.
Decide that you need, and value, the contributions of others, so that
your own thinking can be tested, shaped and stretched. This will
support the improvement of the meeting as a whole.

Believe that everyone attending has something to contribute with so in your next meeting take some time to:

- **Wonder:** about the experiences and knowledge of those around you.
- **Explore:** what they know and how they think.
- **Contrast:** with how that is the same or different to you.
- **Feel glad:** for the fresh air of different perspectives.
- **Gather:** knowledge, insight, wisdom, fact and opinion – then grow.

If you really want to have meetings that achieve and deliver, create space for the others there with you: their words, and the spaces and meaning between their words.

TYPICAL MEETING ROLES

"All the world's a stage, and all the men and women merely players."
Shakespeare, As You Like It

THE MEETING OWNER

The meeting owner is the person who calls for the meeting to take place. Is that you?
As a meeting owner you have a big responsibility.

Compare these two meeting owners:

GEORGE

- Sees a challenge or opportunity.
- Announces "we need a meeting to discuss this".
- Asks somebody to arrange the meeting and send out invitations.
- Makes an agenda which is a timed list of items.
- Calls the meeting in 30-minute blocks, for example, 30 minutes, one hour, two hours, half a day.
- Circulates the agenda.
- Books a meeting room.
- Turns up to the meeting with great hopes and dives in hoping everyone else will too.

CEDRIC

- Thinks "we're facing a challenge or opportunity, I can't do this alone".
- Recognizes that he needs thinking partners.
- Focuses on the purpose of the meeting and uses that as the basis to invite people with the appropriate knowledge and experience (the brains he needs to work with).
- Considers who will be a good naïve resource (somebody to ask the obvious questions).
- Invites each person and explains why he needs them there.
- Decides to 'get at' the challenge (rather than 'get around it') and figures out which conversations need to be had in the meeting.
- Puts the conversations into a sensible sequence and works out how much time each one will need .
- Double-checks that these conversations will serve the overall purpose, to avoid getting knocked off track.
- Considers the possible decisions, and prepares an explanation for how decisions will be made.
- Welcomes the group and thanks them for being with him.
- Frames the meeting by sharing the big purpose, the outcomes to be achieved, the conversations to be had and how decisions will be made.
- Asks each person to introduce themselves and explain their purpose and role in the meeting.
- Ensures everyone dives in together.

And that's it: the touch-paper has been lit: watch that meeting fly!

My provocation to you as a meeting owner is to be more like Cedric; be more intentional. Even if you think you already have it nailed, recognize where you could be smarter.

Twist the Meeting Kaleidoscope to be clear about:

- Why you're bringing people to this space.
- What they need to discuss.
- How best to have discussions.

Then look at the people you want to engage, and create space for them to bring and be their very best.

Here are a few good guideline questions to help you to sharpen up:

- **Why do I need to call this meeting?**
- **What is the compelling focus or purpose of the meeting?**
- **What is the 'straight-line fit' with the bigger goals and purpose of our organization?**
- **What is possible with these people together in a room that wouldn't be possible if they were apart?**
- **What are the big issues that need to be discussed?**
- **How can I engage every brain so that the meeting as a whole is the best that it can be?**
- **How can I focus the group for the whole meeting?**
- **How long do I actually need the meeting to last? (no more gratuitous hours or half-days)**
- **Should I invite a naive resource?**

STRATEGY MEETING

OUTCOME

AGREEMENT ON 5 YEAR PLAN

AGENDA

- WELCOME
- SETTING THE SCENE
- WHERE HAVE WE COME FROM?
- WHERE ARE WE NOW?
- WHERE DO WE NEED TO BE?
- HOW WILL WE GET THERE?

WAYS OF WORKING

- HEALTHY CHALLENGE
- FOCUS

An orientation chart like this will help you to share this thinking with the group. Keeping this visible in the meeting room will serve as a constant focus and guide.

THE MEETING PARTICIPANT

The meeting participant is a person who attends, participates or takes part in the meeting. Is that you? If the meeting owner is not clear about the purpose and goals of the meeting, or is not able to give a compelling reason why you need to be there, be bold and politely decline.

As an aside: I find that the term 'delegate' is often used when referring to meeting participants. This is a word used by hotels and conference centres to mean 'bodies present'. I urge you to use the term 'participant' because it describes, in one word, the act of taking part. Please delete the word 'delegate' from your meeting vocabulary and shift your focus from bodies present to human beings; being humans.

Are you a meeting participant? How would you describe yourself in a meeting? Do you contribute? Do your contributions add value? Are you bound up in your own 'performance'? What do you pay attention to?

Here's a description of a meeting with which I'm familiar:

Every Monday morning the group arrives at the meeting room for a 9am start. By 9.10am everyone is seated in the same seats as the week before (the start time creeps later and later as people drift in, make coffee and small talk).

There's George: the boss. He controls everything. He sits at the head of the table.

There's Kim: she's new to the business. She's taken on a big role in the organization. She sees these meetings as her opportunity to make herself heard – and she does. She seems to express her thinking clearly and appears focused. She sat in George's seat on her first day but soon learned "that's not the way we do things around here".

There's Max: he was 'the voice in the room' before Kim arrived – now he's feeling wrong-footed and is stumbling to regain his place.

There's Michael: he dreads these meetings because he never feels able to find the words quickly enough to express what's in his head. He wants to. His head says – "speak out, say something" – but the conversation moves on and he misses opportunity after opportunity. Whenever he does make a contribution, he begins with "I'm sorry, but...."

There's the quiet guy: what's his name? – he said something once in the meeting but everyone soon recovered.

There's Brie: she's like an eager puppy who wants to impress Max. But now that Kim has arrived, she sees a new opportunity to further her career.

I could go on but I hope you're already getting it.

It is best to remember that: every person attending a meeting has their own unique perspective – their own map of the world – their own reality.

In a good meeting: those unique perspectives find connections and are focused towards the purpose and goal of the meeting.

In a poor meeting: those perspectives are being created all over the place, doing their own thing – clashing, overlapping, confusing, dominating, hiding.

Typically, a poor meeting is the result if the individuals:

- Use it as a platform to be seen and heard (rather than to contribute, understand and be understood).
- Are there because their boss told them to attend (rather than being clear about why and how their contribution serves the meeting purpose).
- Attend because we always do this on a Monday at 9am – "I'm not sure exactly why but it's how we start the week".

Recognize yourself? Recognize others?

Here's an alternative way of thinking about and preparing for a meeting:

- Stop 'blaming' the meeting owner or the other people around the meeting table – that's the lazy way out.
- When you receive a meeting invite:
  - o ask to understand the big purpose of the meeting and what it aims to achieve in the time dedicated to it.
  - o ask why your contribution is important and what expectation there is of you.
- Arrive five minutes early to say your hellos, get your coffee and be ready to begin on time.
- Be prepared to create a positive, intentional experience (map) that frees your mind and those of others.
- Be ready to hear and be heard.
- Make this commitment to yourself and to the group.

THE EXPERT

The expert is the person with a greater level of knowledge in a particular area, for example, the market, the technology, the customer, the numbers, the people.

"Even the peerless sword master Miyamoto Musashi entered the fighting square to learn as much as to teach"

Stephen Pressfield, *Turning Pro*

Is that you? How do you show up? How do you wear your expertise? How do you share what you know?

Compare these two approaches:
Be honest with yourself.

Think:	Think:
I'm the expert, I know more about this than others here: knowledge is power	I wonder how I can help this group with what I know
	Feel:
Feel:	Desire to help
Superior to the rest	
	Do:
Do:	Ask "what would be most helpful?"
Give information sparingly on a need-to-know basis	Add insight, knowledge and experience when required
	Learn as much as I teach

As you think about the way you bring your expertise to meetings, please also consider whether you're type-casting yourself into that role and becoming a caricature. You know what I mean: the numbers girl with the serious expression or the operations guy who "just wants a plan", and so on.

Here's a great twist: the most memorable experts I have come across in meetings are those who are the most flexible.

For example, I know a finance director who is so focused on getting the most from the team that she ably facilitates their meetings while also contributing numbers, forecasts, critical thinking.

I know a logistics and supply chain director who champions people development as much as the raw material to delivery process.

I know a HR manager who rigorously and purposefully connects the people talent strategy with the organization's purpose, strategy and bottom line.

No type-casting with these three. Yes, they are experts in their chosen field and they know their stuff, yet they consciously flex their knowledge and contributions in meetings to maximize the conversation, for the sake of the whole.

Do you?

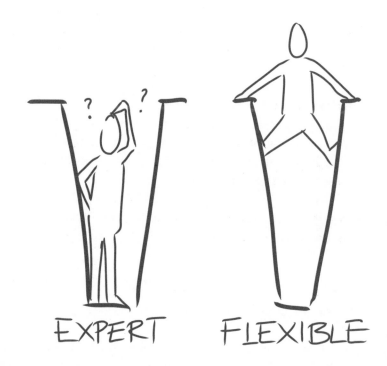

EXPERT   FLEXIBLE

THE CHAIRPERSON

This role is most commonly used in institutions and committees where a person is required to preside over a meeting in an orderly and structured fashion. The chairperson helps ensure the meeting and its participants observe the rules and governance required by the organization.

I think that chairpersons get a bad press. I was one once – it was tough because there were strict rules by which to abide and very little leeway or freedom to deviate. It's a challenging job – unless you thrive on control and command – in which case, you might love it! It is a hierarchical role without a lot of room for flexibility. You have to be good at gently wielding a rod of iron. You enable order, structure, routine, minutes and rigour.

It's not for all and yet it is a very important role.

In many ways, the role of a chairperson is very different from that of the other meeting roles. However, it still comes down to the same structure of any good meeting, so that a chairperson's role is made simpler with:

- A clear meeting purpose.
- Clear rules and roles.
- Purposeful agenda items.
- Defined timing and process.

THE FACILITATOR

*"Facilitation is a way of being. It is not an add-on tool or
a performance, or act, or 'something to get out of the bag'.
It is a way of being with people such that the outcome of
the connected parts and the whole are enhanced"*
> Catherine Hennessy, director, The Facilitation Partnership

What is a good facilitator?

1. A good facilitator believes the group has the answer or knows how to find the answer and they work with the group to unlock it. This is very important since the more a group learns how to unlock and share its own knowledge and insight, the more effective it becomes.
2. Good facilitation supports individuality and independence within the group rather than them depending on the facilitator.
3. A good facilitator knows that success in a meeting is not about their 'performance', rather, it's about the group's result and resulting action.
4. Good facilitation enables effective conversation, decision-making, planning and execution.
5. A good facilitator believes that facilitation can happen anywhere, quickly, live and in the moment; that it simply requires conscious thought plus knowledge and skill.
6. A good facilitator believes that authenticity is the difference that makes the difference. Good facilitation cannot be faked.

Facilitation is also a leadership competence. While it can be used in formal meeting settings it should not be confined to that space. It is a waste of skill if it is saved only for the meeting room.

It is worth noting that the best facilitators are the ones who are content-agnostic. They care about you having the right conversations but they don't contribute to them. They simply, carefully, expertly and wisely hold the group in a safe crucible of conversation while they attend to the process of enabling conversation.

A word of advice – a good facilitator will:
- **Explore the situation and context around your meeting to understand how it fits into the wider business picture.**
- **Help you to clarify the specific goals for the meeting.**
- **Speak to participants to understand their personal requirements and expectations.**
- **Build an agenda to achieve the meeting goals.**
- **Prepare the materials needed to support the agenda.**
- **Facilitate with confidence, flexibility and care on the day to achieve the goals agreed.**
- **Provide a record of the meeting to use for follow-up and communication.**

'Now that we've named some of the roles involved in meetings we stand a chance of overcoming them. Yes, overcoming them. Here's the news – no matter which chair you sit in, no matter what capacity you arrive in, it's your job to make sure this meeting is a success. Come on. It's time to make a change. To evolve; adapt; to communicate; to get things done; to enjoy those conversations.'

NEWSFLASH

DIFFERENT PREFERENCES FOR GETTING THINGS DONE

"Strength lies in differences not in similarities"

Stephen R Covey, educator and author

As you sit down at your next meeting, take a look around the table. Be conscious in those first few moments of the reality of who's there. You may see the usual, known faces or you may be in a meeting with people for the first time. Whatever the combination, you can be certain that each person will have their own preference for getting things done.

Around the table there will be:

DETAIL HUNTERS

· "Detail hunters" – the people who like the facts (and as little fluff as possible).

· "Big picture thinkers" – the people who like to consider what's possible.

BIG PICTURE THINKERS

- People who thrive on schedules, plans and deadlines.

- Those who prefer to keep their options open for as long as possible.

What is your preference for getting things done? Perhaps that all depends on what's being discussed; sometimes you like the facts, sometimes you like the possibilities of the big picture, and so on.

Your preference shifts and so do the preferences of others. The shifts in preference happen for many reasons ranging from your interest in the subject, to the day of the week or time of the day.

Here you have it: lots of diverse preferences and styles all sitting in the same meeting and (apparently) all focusing on the same thing. At times, having such a diverse combination of people involved can feel like survival of the fittest. It can often be the case that the most articulate, dogmatic or political person is heard over everyone else. With so many styles of communication, and so many preferences, you may wonder whether you will ever be able to please everyone.

Mercifully, no two people are the same – and therein lies the opportunity.

So you can stop hoping that Sarah will not be 'difficult' by asking too many detailed questions; stop expecting that Simon will want time to think; and that Jim will want to explore all possibilities, and so on.

Use what you know about people's preferences to plan your meeting.

About yourself, consider these questions:
- **"What do I know for sure about this subject?"**
- **"What am I assuming?"**
- **"What are the possible options?"**
- **"What question am I trying to answer here?"**
- **"What's my aim?"**

About others, consider these questions:
- **"How can I help them hear each other?"**
- **"Where do they seem to be agreeing?"**
- **"What could be their point of difference?"**
- **"How can I help them know what is fact and what is assumption?"**

By posing and considering these questions you will add rigour to the conversations in your meetings. If you don't know the people in a meeting well enough to plan for their preferences, you can safely assume there will be the full range, so plan accordingly by having a clear and shared purpose with each person knowing why their personal contribution is needed.

Above all – remember that your working preference is one among many, and that's good because as you learn to flex with others your own ability will develop.

LABELS AND THINGS

"Who's the fish?"

> The waiter in our local restaurant.

It's funny what a chair can do to people!

It's funny what a meeting and a room can do to people!

Many people treat and speak about meetings as a 'thing'. Do you?

"I'm in *a meeting*." "I've got *back-to-back meetings*."

People then 'out-meeting' one another: "I'll take your *meeting* and raise it. I've got more, bigger, tougher, more stressful meetings than you." The "my cat is blacker than your cat" syndrome.

And, as if 'thing-ing' a meeting isn't enough, I've seen perfectly sane people walk over a meeting room threshold and transform into the meeting versions of themselves to become gladiators in an arena; or part of a heckling crowd; or a silent witness; or a fierce lion; or the shuffling pack; or a grumpy old man.... and in doing so, turning themselves into caricatures of themselves.

Then labels are attached – just like that:

- He's an **introvert** who never speaks.
- She's an **extrovert**, you can't shut her up.

- He's **"always difficult"** – he throws in the curved balls just as we think we've agreed something and opens it all back up again.
- He's the **joker** – he tries to diffuse tricky discussions by throwing in comments to make everyone laugh.
- She's the **expert** and knows everything about this.

Do you "thing" people by putting labels on them?

Think about the assumptions attached to the labels you have given people. How do these assumptions and labels lead you to behave? Do you cut some people short, while having plenty of time for others? Perhaps you switch off when the person who contributes most begins to speak (there she goes again, blah, blah blah!)? Or perhaps you listen intently when the most senior person in the room has something to say (got to be seen to be interested)?

Do you attach a label to somebody and then back it up with a statement about them that is stated as a hard fact:

- He's from finance (label), he always wants the detail (assumed fact).
- She's an extrovert (label), nobody else will get a word in (assumed fact).
- He's one of those creative types (label), he'll want to see it in pictures (assumed fact).
- She's from HR (label), she'll want to know how we all feel about this (assumed fact).

What's crazy is that people seem to comply and become the label they've been given. It's like a tacit understanding of "I know my place"; "I know my role"; "I know what you expect of me"; "I'll comply because it's what's expected".

What label have you given yourself in meetings? How does that make you behave? I wonder what label others have put on you......

Labelling and thing-ing happens in meeting rooms all over the world. It happens in other places too, such as restaurants, hospitals, train stations, airports, banks, car parks – you name it – it's rife.

I remember being told this example of thing-ing – it made me laugh then and it still makes me smile to this day. Picture the scene:

You are with a friend in a restaurant.
You call for the menu – the menu arrives. Actually, a human being brings you the menu, but you think, "ah, here's the menu!" – as though it had a life of its own.

You want to order, you call the waiter – and you probably have all kinds of labels about the people who serve you.

"I'll have the beef."
"I'll have the fish."

Later, when the waiter brings you the food you ordered it's his turn to 'thing' you:

"Who's the fish?"
(you comply) *"I'm the fish."*
Yep, you are!

Same in hospital.
"Aaahhh – so Mrs Smith, you're the appendix."

With wild abandon we label introverts, extroverts, thinkers, feelers, – and so the list goes on.

While I am a fan of some personality-type indicators (Myers Briggs in particular), I often notice people in organizations getting stuck on the labels rather than their meaning, and that has a direct effect on how they engage with each other.

I know. I get it. Labels are a sort of shorthand and we all know what we mean, right?

Maybe.

The trouble is, when we 'thing' and label one another, we forget there's a human being on the other side of the fish, the appendix, the introvert, the extrovert – and it is limiting to de-humanize people in this way. For example, just because a person prefers to reflect before contributing doesn't mean they never speak or are slow – it's just that they want time to consider. So, give them time to consider!

And, before you think "yeah yeah – you don't know our office", believe me, I do. You can do better. You can get even more from yourself and even more from one another. Human to human, rather than thing to thing or label to label.

At your next meeting, know this:

A little bit of knowledge about personality types does not mean you should put labels on yourself and others.

At your next meeting, try this:

1. Look beyond the labels, look at each individual human being.
2. View each person as a unique individual and ask yourself "what am I bringing to this?"; "how am I showing up?; "what can I do to contribute better?"
3. Notice your routine in putting a label on somebody else.
4. Reframe your thinking from "introvert" or "extrovert" to "Michael" or "Susan".
5. Ask yourself "what am I doing to help that human being feel heard and understood?"

Stop thinking about your meetings as "things" – start thinking about them as their component parts:

- **the purpose of the meeting**
- **the people in the meeting**
- **the process of the meeting**
- **the content being shared**

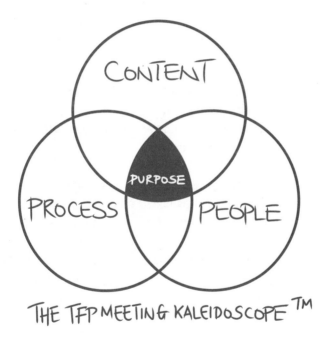

THE TFP MEETING KALEIDOSCOPE ™

If you adopt this thinking, the next time you step into a meeting room you'll notice your meeting behaviours become much more people-focused and you'll be more likely to get what you want and need from the meeting.

TRUST AND RESPECT

Here's a true story.

A girl dreamed that she stepped into a school gymnasium. She looked up and saw her friend – also a member of her team – at the top of a rope holding on. She looked again and screamed to the others "quick, grab the mats, she's holding her own rope!"

What she had seen in her bizarre dream vision was her friend at the top of the rope, but the rope wasn't attached to anything; she had seen that her friend was in a very precarious and dangerous position and was wholly counting on her own strength, determination and ability to hold the top of the rope.

It turned out that her friend was indeed struggling to find support in this team. Although she was putting a brave face on things, she couldn't work out how she fitted into the team and was feeling alone.

Calling a team, a "team", in the true sense of the word, means little if the people inside the team feel alone or that they're holding their own ropes.

I hear many stories about meetings where communication breaks down due to lack of trust. One person told me, "I attended a meeting where something of a discussion took place. Some people had a pop at each other and then we all came out of the meeting. As we walked along the corridor I asked the chap next to me "what did we decide?" There was no answer..." The people in that meeting were none the wiser about what had been discussed, they just knew that there had been a disagreement without a clear outcome.

Some say that if trust and respect exists within a team, then disagreements can happen and most things can be shared. Yet, the truth is that if trust is not established, what we think and what we say can be worlds apart.

It is worth considering how much trust there is among the people in your meetings. If you feel it is lacking, here are some suggestions that may help:

- **Agree a shared goal that everyone can contribute to.**
- **Make sure people know why their contribution is important.**
- **Speak with, not past, or at, one another.**
- **Be curious to understand the opinions and thinking behind the points exchanged.**
- **Listen well and seek to understand.**

Notice that the words 'like each other' do not appear in this list. The good news is that you don't all have to like one another to be able to do good work in meetings. In fact, many groups and teams are able to thrive in a trusting environment simply because they have mutual respect and a shared goal.

EXISTING TEAM AND A NEW TEAM LEADER

Good team leaders know when..... that's it, they just know when. Whether they lead, follow, decide, share, tell, shape, speak, remain silent – they just know when.

I observe leaders take over an existing team.

I watch good leaders explore the why, what and how of the existing team. They get alongside for a while to understand what's working and where things could be sharper. Then they work with the team to create a refined focus, shape and rhythm.

I watch the not-so-good leaders arrive and say "all change": new focus, new shape, new rhythm. They overlay their own meeting routines and practices and expect people to "get with the programme."

If you have recently acquired an existing team, please pause and take stock before changing the meetings, rhythms and patterns that you've inherited. They might be working just fine. You don't have to change the meeting routine just to establish your leadership. The team are already in transition and getting used to you as their new boss, so their existing meeting can act as an important anchor for a team. If they're already working well, they act as stabilizers which in turn will help to steady the environment.

On the other hand, if the existing meeting rhythm and practice is not working so well, get the team's suggestions and support in making changes.

Before any changes are made, the whole team should take a look at:

- The purpose of these meetings.
- What you can do together in meetings that you cannot do apart.
- Why, specifically, these meetings work / don't work.
- How decisions are made.
- If decisions lead to clear action (or fall apart in the car park).

The team will soon let you know what works and what doesn't.

The insights you share will help you to see what needs sharpening and why. It could be that the biggest and best thing you could do is to get alongside them and support a way of meeting that works.

In the first few weeks of leading an existing team, focus on supporting the momentum they have – don't get in the way of it because of your need to lead. You'll find, in this way, you'll earn trust quickly which will help you to build shared understanding. A great foundation for shaping an aligned way of working in the months to come.

This section puts the spotlight on the unsung hero of meetings:
that is, the way people engage with the content.

Stop the timed lists.

Start using engaging process instead.

A good process is the golden key that will unlock your meetings
and ensure that they achieve and deliver, every time.

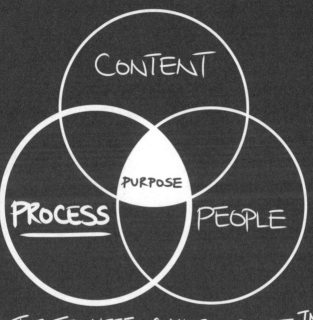

PART FOUR

THE TFP MEETING KALEIDOSCOPE ™

TWIST 3

PROCESS

MEETINGS ARE UNSTABLE ENTITIES

*"No man ever steps in the same river twice,
for it's not the same river and he's not the same man"*

Heraclitus, Ancient Greek philosopher

Consider my earlier suggestion that meetings are alive (with human beings, teams, groups, co-workers, managers, and so on). Being alive means movement (large and small), energy (high and low), shifting (in every direction; side to side and up and down). It's all going on in your meeting.

Think about it, in one meeting alone:

- Time moves.
- Understanding shifts.
- Relationships strengthen and weaken.
- Agreements are reached and then broken.
- Stamina and resilience are tested.
- Hunger comes and goes.
- Sugar levels rise and fall.

And let's not forget those wandering and unruly minds.

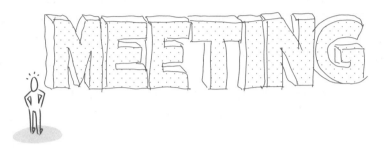

These elements are continually changing in their forms and shapes. Some are clear to see and some are invisible to the human eye.

I agree with the Greek philosopher Heraclitus in so much as the components of any meeting change continually; just like that flowing river, you can't step into the same meeting twice. Even with the same people present, there is instability in the system of a meeting: it is inevitable.

This, in my opinion, is one of the reasons why meetings can feel like straight-jackets as they attempt to bring 'control' and 'order'– their intention is to be efficient, but their impact can be to stifle and limit what is possible.

There is another way.

Rather than trying to control and inhibit the energy of the unstable meeting environment, you can work with it to maximize potential to make a significant shift in the efficacy of meetings.

Just as a dancer feels the rhythm in a piece of music, you can learn to dance with style in meetings. By all means have your planned choreography (a known set of moves), but ensure you are free in the moment to respond to unexpected beats and bars, with responsive twists and turns.

Twist the Meeting Kaleidoscope to vary your approach to bring the very best out in an unstable environment. Consider this:

- **The purpose of the meeting** – the steady and stable core – share it, have it visible, use it to help keep conversations on track.
- **The people in the meeting** – flesh and blood, a combination of certainty and insecurity – support each one to be heard and support each one to be understood.
- **The process of the meeting** – be clear about which conversation points will serve the purpose, give space and time for those conversations to happen.
- **The content being shared** – welcome opinion as well as fact – make sure it serves the purpose and enlightens people.

THE MEETING TRANCE

And... back in the room...

Yes, back in that meeting room.

Back in that seat.

With the same view.

With the same set up.

With the same old wonky flip-chart stand.

With the interactive whiteboard that only a few people know how to use (when it's working).

With the PowerPoint slides.

With the same routine.

With the...with the...with the...

And... back in the room.

DO SOMETHING DIFFERENT.

Do you understand me?

Enough said.

STRAIGHT JACKETS
AND COMFY JUMPERS

"So high, I can't get over it
So low, I can't get under it
So wide, I can't get 'round it"

Peter, Paul and Mary, Oh, Rock My Soul

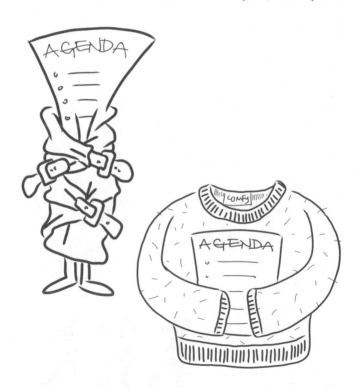

People are in meetings all over the word, right at this exact moment. Each gathered group is doing what it can to plan something, solve it, create it, connect it, get around it, pre-empt it, overcome it, align it – I could go on.

Even with the assumption that a clear purpose exists and that the right people are in the room (which is frequently not the case), there are two further things that can get in the way of a successful meeting:

- The length of the agenda is often way too long with far too many items crammed into a timed list.
- An expectation that we will move from one agenda item to the next without considering *how* each item on the agenda could be approached.

Try this:
1. **Reduce the number of items on your upcoming agenda by half and include only those topics that require exploration and/or a decision by the group.**
2. **Approach each agenda item with a process to help reach a purposeful outcome.**

Here are a couple of caricatures that depict 'typical meetings' to illustrate what I mean. (Note that these caricatures are used to demonstrate these scenarios in an extreme manner so that you can react to them as observations and then perhaps compare them to your meetings).

THE STRAIGHT-JACKET MEETING

"We gotta get through this...."

These meetings can usually be found in hierarchical organizations, or parts of organizations, where tight (or reasonably tight) control is required or habitual. The routine goes something like:

Agenda:

- Minutes and actions from last meeting.
- First agenda item (that didn't get covered last time).
- Second agenda item (that didn't get covered last time).
- Third agenda item.
- Fourth agenda item.
- Fifth agenda item.
- Sixth agenda item.
- Seventh agenda item.
- Eighth agenda item – no time to cover this, move to next week.
- Ninth agenda item – let's jump to this quickly and make a fast decision.
- Tenth agenda item (that didn't get covered last time and is still at the bottom of the list).
- Eleventh agenda item – the Christmas party.

PROS:

- Can be good for sharing information.
- Liked by people with a preference for routine and structure ("we know where we are in this meeting and somebody is taking control").

CONS:

- Discussion and exploration is often limited.
- Rigidity and order can be frustrating for some participants.

In my experience, straight-jacket meetings tend to be the ones that result in least action being taken on decisions made. In fact, many of the decisions made in these meetings are frequently questioned afterwards and have to be revisited in the next meeting.

THE COMFY JUMPERS MEETING

"We're all over the place."

The routine goes something like this:

People arrive more or less on time (perhaps they're a little late because they're so busy going from one meeting to the next – and by the way, they can't stay until the end because need to get to the next meeting). The first 15 minutes tends to be spent in conversation not related to the agenda and this is followed by "ahem, let's focus on the meeting", which is then followed by a meandering, unstructured, discussion that gets easily knocked off-track into side conversations.

PROS:

- Lends itself to spontaneity which can lead to creative thinking.

CONS:

- Can feel aimless and loose.
- Frustrates some participants due to the lack of structure.

Neither of the two approaches caricatured is wrong, per se. However, following the same old routine does limit what could be possible.

The way to sharpen up either one of these approaches is by:

- Having, and sharing, a crystal-clear purpose and goal; one that is connected to your organization's purpose and goal for each meeting (I know I'm banging on about this – but I need you to hear it).
- Being realistic about what you can discuss in the time available and focusing only on those things in the meeting.
- Sharing information before the meeting; this should be prepared in headline form, in a two-page document at the most. You should also let everyone attending the meeting know where they can find more context or background so that they can research further if required (this will avoid the cop out that "people won't read it").
- Be prepared for a conversation on the pre-read material when people are together in the room.

Although the 'straight jacket' and 'comfy jumper' approaches have served many meetings well, there are many other more productive and engaging approaches available that demonstrate HOW meeting conversations can and should happen.

AGENDA DESIGN PART 1

THE OVERARCHING FRAMEWORK

"I believe the answers are in the room, we just need to design this meeting to help the team to explore and there we will find them"
Ben Robinson, director, The Facilitation Partnership

Choosing the best way to support each agenda item is like a golfer selecting the best club for a hole, or an athlete choosing the right trainers for a workout. Simply put, you have to choose the best tools for the job.

Remember the truths about unstable environments and unruly, wandering minds? You must plan to work with both. Choosing a good process won't necessarily guarantee you success, but it will get you further than using a putter to drive off a par four.

First, think in terms of "conversations to be had" rather than "agenda items". This shift will help you to reframe how you think about meetings and to approach them in a more resourceful way.

Then, ask yourself which series of conversations need to be had in service of the purpose and goal. Break down those conversations further into smaller, bite-sized steps to make them easier to plan and organize.

Now, design the process of the meeting with clarity of purpose, goals and the conversations to be had.

How to do it?

There are two, distinct layers of good agenda design:

1. The overarching framework
2. The step-by-step process

EXAMPLES OF OVERARCHING FRAMEWORKS:

4 Dimensions Framework

I put this framework together after many years of learning to understand work in groups. It has become a good standby and works for me in most instances.

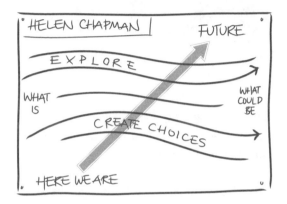

- Welcome and connect everyone.
- Orientate to why we're here and what we need to achieve together.
- Explore each topic area using simple process tools.
- Create choices.
- Explore options, giving the pros and cons of each option.
- Decide which options to go with.
- Create a plan to achieve them.

G.R.O.W. – the coaching framework inspired by the framework made popular in McKinsey by Graham Alexander. I find that this structure works beautifully as a framework for a meeting.

- What is our **Goal** for this topic area?
- What is our current **Reality** in this topic area?
- Based on what we know, what **Options** do we have?
- What **Will** we commit to doing next?

PAST, PRESENT, FUTURE, PLAN – inspired by the Strategic Vision-ing process developed by David Sibbet, president and founder of The Grove Consultants International:

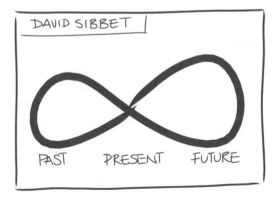

- What lessons have we learned from our history?
- Where are we today? What is real for us now?
- What's the boldest, brightest future we can imagine?
- What are the big steps to get us there from where we've been and where we find ourselves today?
- What's our plan to get there?

Participatory Decision Making – inspired by the work of Sam Kaner's, author of *The Facilitator's Guide to Participatory Decision Making*.

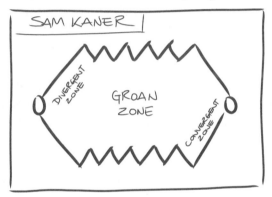

- Opening: open to the conversation with reason and purpose.
- Working: discuss and explore options.
- Stretching: hold discussions open for longer to ensure all angles are explored.
- Deciding: decide the best route to take.
- Moving: plan to move on that decision.

As the strength of a building begins with a solid foundation and steel structure, so the key to good meeting design begins with a good overarching framework. It will be strong enough to support the step-by-step processes you add to it.

AGENDA DESIGN
PART 2

GOING BEYOND THE FLIPCHART LIST

"Working visually will empower the group (and individuals) to generate meaning and ideas as the conversation progresses, leading to insights that otherwise may not have been encountered"

Tom Russell, director, Inky Thinking

Once you have chosen the overarching framework, you can begin the second stage of meeting design. These steps are the smaller, moment-by-moment moves that will bring the overarching framework to life.

Orientation chart – Great for focusing and refocusing the group on the meeting purpose, goals, agenda and ways of working.

Clustered sticky note chart – Great for gathering ideas and sorting into groups to spot both popular and outlier thinking.

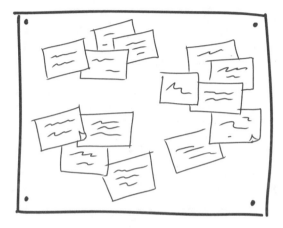

Mind maps – Great for building up and connecting emergent thinking.

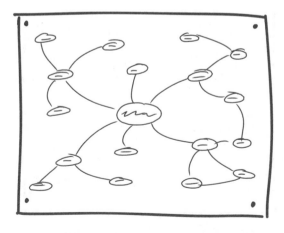

Lists – Great for a quick and spontaneous 'download' of ideas and data.

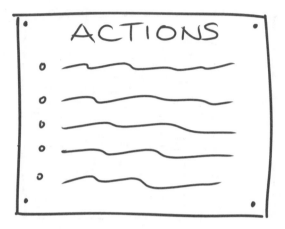

Compare and contrast – Great for comparing and cross referencing combinations of data to support decisions.

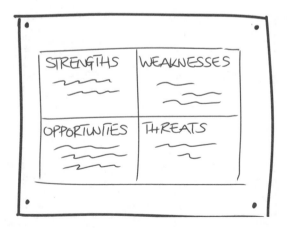

Process diagrams – Great for identifying how something does or might work, such as a business process.

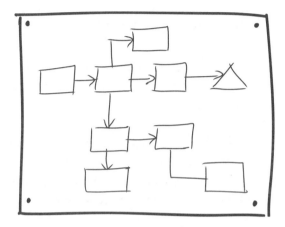

Drawing – Great for bringing an idea, concept, challenge or opportunity visually to life in any way you like.

FAST MEETINGS

HOW FAST DO YOU WANT IT TO BE?

Fast, focused and efficient meetings are becoming the norm in smart businesses such that meeting rooms are used only when in-depth exploration needs to happen.

Your meetings can be portable and fast – anytime, anyplace, anywhere and suggest you use fast meetings for decision making when you know that most of the group or team members are already up to speed with context of the matters being discussed.

Here is the overarching framework:
Meet > Fast Focus > Decide > Commit > Leave

Here is an example step-by-step process design:

Before
- Be clear about the intended goal for the meeting, in advance.
- Agree on a time to finish the meeting, in advance so that everyone knows the focused intentionality of the meeting.

During
- Stand, don't sit.
- Fast Focus by saying "as you know by the end of this 20 minutes we must achieve X".
- State the context clearly and tell the group what clarification they need.
- Provide known options and ask for other options not yet shared.
- Use a timed go-around process to hear everyone's view / preference.
- Narrow to an either/or based on what we know and gut feel.
- One person calls the final decision (the boss perhaps?).
- Agree on action required with a timeline / deadline.
- Finish as a soon as everything has been covered – there is no need to linger.

MEET > FAST FOCUS > DECIDE > COMMIT > LEAVE

This sounds simple, but it needs practice. You'll go through the conscious layers of learning until it becomes second nature, and you'll be glad that you did.

PROCESS:
A WORD OF CAUTION!

IF YOU USE THE SAME TECHNIQUE AND PROCESS IN EVERY MEETING YOU'RE BEING LAZY

Just because a process worked well for you once, doesn't mean you can, or should, hit people with it time and time again. A meeting process should always serve the need of people to have the conversation they need to have. So just because mind-mapping worked well last time, it doesn't mean you should do it again and again.

I recently had a conversation with Jack Beadle, a professional chef that sums up this point perfectly. We were speaking about the priceless nature of raw ingredients and how every carrot, potato and banana shallot has done its bit by growing to the best of its ability. It then arrives on the chefs chopping board ready for its big moment.

The way I see it, there are four ideas that chefs hold to be true:

1. Cooking is an art form – art is affected by mood.
2. Chefs have to 'show up', be present, be prepared to be there and nowhere else from the preparation to the service itself – every time, hour after hour.
3. Each and every raw ingredient is to be respected.
4. Each and every raw ingredient is unique.

No two banana shallots are identical, and while a chef can rely on muscle memory when chopping one, he cannot chop the next one in exactly the same way. If he tried that he would be being lazy. A lazy chef will chop his fingers off.

He must make subtle changes and adaptions for every single shallot.

Here's the comparison that I hold to be true:

1. Meetings are an art form – they are affected by mood.
2. You have to 'show-up', be present, be prepared to be there and nowhere else from the start to the finish – every time.
3. Each and every person in that meeting is to be respected.
4. Each and every person is unique.

If you use the same technique and process for every meeting you're being lazy. True, you might not chop off your fingers, but neither will you maximize the possibilities on that day.

Flex and change your meeting's process design to meet the shifting needs of the group, conversation and goal. For example, you might try:

- Varying whole group conversation with small groups or pairs.
- Making space for quiet reflection after information has been shared so that people have time to think about what they want to say or ask.

A varied meeting process will help to bring content to life, so rather than having everyone sitting around the meeting table, wading their way through an agenda, try:

- Contrasting discussion sessions with personal reflection.
- Mixing up the whole group sessions with individual or paired reflection.

The trick to a well-designed process for a meeting is to:

- **Decide on the big, overarching structure of the meeting, for example, G.R.O.W.**
- **Focus on a goal for each conversation, for example, an agreement, five big ideas, or a plan.**
- **Decide how to get people involved in the meeting discussions.**
- **Consider styles and preferences.**

TEMPUS FUGIT

MEETINGS ARE ABOUT TO GET SHORTER, SHARPER AND MORE FOCUSED

Do you call meetings in the usual big blocks of time? For example, 30 minutes; one hour; two hours; half a day; a whole day; two days, etc?

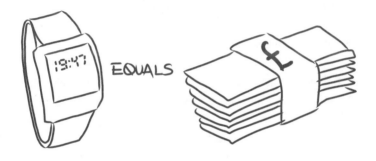

A conversation I had with friends turned to our respective futures and the choices we all face about important areas of our lives. As we paused to reflect on the decisions that lay ahead, one friend commented that if 83 years is the average span of human life, that equates to 996 months. I quickly did the maths only to realize that (if I'm lucky) I have just 360 months to go. Not long is it? You might imagine I left the conversation feeling a little daunted that my life on the planet is trickling like sand through the hourglass of life. On the contrary, I left feeling energized beyond belief. There is no escaping the fact that our time here is brief and it's down to each of us to make the most of it alongside the people we care about most.

The truth is that we live face-to-face with time. It is our worst enemy and our best friend. I hear people say they are "time poor" and that they are searching for balance. This is true in personal lives and it is true in business lives as well, where hour upon hour is spent in meetings, preparing for meetings, travelling to meetings, tinkering with technology for meetings. Time is a commodity that requires fine tuning and balance.

Now, think about how you call meetings using those usual big time blocks. Add up the hours. Add up the costs. Now balance that with the return on investment of those meetings – whether that return is in the form of turnover, profit, relationships or shared knowledge. Are you really getting value?

Become thrifty with time. When meetings are planned in chunks of one hour, it's like rounding up your cash to the nearest £1, £10, £100 when you pay for something. That would be a waste of your money and you'd be mad to do it.

Become conscious about the value of time by making your meetings more focussed and much simpler. Give yourself and others enough time in your meetings to do what is required, and then give time back.

Think about the time in your next meeting that way. Be crystal clear about what the meeting should achieve. Design the meeting process to suit the time available. Don't be lazy by blocking out an hour for this or half a day for that – do the maths and figure out the appropriate time that is required, be focused. Allow only for the time you need to achieve the required goals – and no more.

WALKING AND TALKING

CONVERSATIONS ARE SOMETIMES BETTER OUTSIDE OF A MEETING ROOM

Must a meeting take place in a room?

One of the best meeting of minds I ever experienced took place overnight. I was wearing sweatpants and a decorated bra (fluorescent pink feathers). It took six hours to complete.

It was one long, perpetual conversation, passed from woman to woman, through the night, fed by encouragement, passion, focus and determination – all taking part in a 42.195 kilometre (26.21875 mile) walk.

It was an experience I'll never forget.

It was a meeting of several thousand participants. They all wanted to be there. They all planned to be there; to be present and nowhere else. There was a compelling purpose – to raise money for a breast cancer charity.

Our meeting room was the streets of London. It happened at night because the 'meeting room' wasn't available during the day. Our purpose was so strong – a missed night's sleep wasn't going to stop us. And then it began – we started to walk. My friend and I held hands for support (and so that we didn't lose each other among the masses) as we marched out of Hyde Park.

Everyone was focused and intentional. I noticed a sound – a steady hum – it was the sound of people talking as they walked. The speed at which my friend and I were walking meant that we passed others or were passed by them as they walked past us. Then a realization came. As we passed, or were passed, we momentarily joined the conversation – we would listen and contribute before moving on – taking that conversation with us – connecting it to next walkers we came to. The hum I could hear came from 15,000 walkers – coming together to achieve something for a compelling purpose, each with a personal goal to contribute fully and make a difference; all spurred on by the conversation being passed along that long, long line.

I offer you the idea of walking and talking is a serious proposition. It is a physiological fact that when the human body is engaged in a known, repetitive activity, the rhythm and cycles of the brain are able to slow down – and when brain waves are slower, there is a greater chance of creativity, deeper thought and insight. That's why you frequently have your best ideas when you're brushing your teeth, taking a shower, washing the car, making a cake, or falling asleep and so on.

Can you get your meetings, or parts of your meetings, to happen outside of a meeting room?

To be clear, I'm not talking about engaging meeting people in 'team activities' that require frenetic thinking, such as treasure hunts, or paint-balling – or anything that requires organized thought. I'm suggesting slowing down everything and building in time to think, to be reflective to allow thinking to slow down?

I'm sure you can think of ways of doing this. I'm sure you can make it a possibility.

A word to the wise – taking your meeting outside requires :

- A compelling purpose – a clear reason to take part.
- A clear understanding of why the contribution of each person is important.
- A clear goal that is connected to the purpose.

Simply put, an actual, physical meeting room can, and sometimes should, be switched for a new environment. The location can create a new perspective (particularly in a recurring discussion). What is most important is the conversations that take place.

IF YOU DO DECIDE TO OPT FOR A MEETING ROOM

Choose a room with:

- Space.
- Natural light.
- Moveable furniture.
- Sufficient flat wall space.
- A well-stocked 'meeting kit' (see below) to support discussion.
- Outside space to give you an option for fresh air.

METAPHORS
IN MEETINGS

YOU DON'T HAVE TO BE A GOOD STORYTELLER
TO DO THIS WELL

For as long as I can remember, I have been drawn to using metaphors to help express my thoughts – they serve my natural propensity to see parallels in situations. You will spot plenty in this book (for example, chefs and shallots, golfers, athletes and so on).

I imagine you hear many metaphors through the course of a day:

- He carried the world on his shoulders.
- We were lost in a sea of information.
- It was like music to my ears.
- My legs were like jelly.

- Her head was spinning with ideas.
- They were like ships passing in the night.

The use of metaphor in conversation can help to describe feelings and explain concepts.

It is for this reason that a conscious use of metaphor in a meeting can serve people well.

Here are some metaphors I've experienced that have been used to support the meeting process:

- **When creating a vision for the future:** using space travel to evoke connections to leadership, belief, behaviour, visions, dreams.
- **When creating a project plan:** choosing the right ingredients and combining them correctly to create something great.
- **When creating a team:** referring to sports teams with the right people in the right positions focused on a plan to succeed.
- **When overcoming challenges:** likening to climbing a mountain, overcoming difficulty, meeting challenges on the path, working as a team to overcome them.
- **When creating harmony and alignment:** using music to describe the rhythm and drumbeat; tempo and pace; people and the organization.
- **When developing strategy:** choosing a journey metaphor to describe the big steps required against the terrain and distance we need to travel.
- **When describing movement in an organization:** describing movement as though in a vehicle, perhaps changing from a steam train to an intercity express as the pace gathers speed.

What can you add to this list?

While I encourage the use of metaphors in your meetings, for maximum impact I urge you to:

- Use them consciously and sparingly.
- Avoid taking them to extremes, for example down to the detail of every nut and bolt in the engine of the space rocket.
- Choose the ones that have a personal impact on you, in that way you will be authentic in sharing them.

MAKING DECISIONS

MAKING CONSCIOUS CHOICES

Nothing can unravel a meeting quicker than failure to focus on how decisions will be made. Moreover if you take a flimsy approach to making decisions you may find that what you thought had been decided in a meeting falls apart in the hours afterwards. The result is that the actions you thought had been agreed fail to take place and you make little or no progress.

Be smart by putting a spotlight on:
* How each conversation will be approached and explored.

and
* How each conversation will be concluded and decided.

Be explicit in every meeting about how decisions will be made – item by item. In this way, people will be ready and equipped to make them, and this will be more likely to result in follow-up and action being taken.

Commonly-used decision-making options include:

* Consensus voting where every single person must agree or disagree.
* Majority voting where most of the people agree or disagree.
* Expert decides where the most knowledgeable person on the subject decides for the group.
* The boss decides on behalf of the group.

Knowing when to make a decision can be hard to spot. To help, you can ask questions such as:

- **What have we missed?**
- **What else should we consider?**
- **Who has a different point?**

Be aware that the right time to make a decision can happen at any time in a conversation, and can sometimes happen earlier than you expected. If the group aligns on something quickly, why wait? Decide, agree action and move on.

But, what if the group has agreed that consensus decision is needed but is divided in opinion?

Here's what to do:

- Create a two-column chart with headings: "what we agree on" and "what we need to discuss further."
- Write in both columns what is relevant in each column.
- You may find that people shift position when they see it written down.
- Allow time for further exploration and encourage everyone to spot alignments and misalignments as they discuss again.
- Ask the participants to be as specific as possible and separate out the facts from opinions – this will support a greater understanding and the decision may come.

Above all, remember to leave enough time and space in your meeting plan to support the process of making decisions – without them the meeting will remain nothing more than a conversation.

VIRTUAL MEETINGS

NEWSFLASH! THEY'RE NOT VIRTUAL AT ALL BECAUSE THEY PHYSICALLY EXIST

"We seem to be spending a lot of time trying to replace humans"
Luke Varda, project consultant

"Hi, it's Susan, I'm going on mute."
"Hi, it's Michael, I'm driving so I'll be on mute."
"Hi, it's Steve, there's a lot of background noise, I'm going on mute."
"Hi, it's Emma, I'm on a train, I'm going on mute."
"Hi, it's Ralph."

What you wanted was five engaged brains on a conference call and what you got was two silent drivers, a harassed mother, somebody finishing a report, somebody in Tesco's car park trying to get a signal. Each person thinking it's acceptable to dial in and announce "I'm going on mute". Each doing so for what they think is reasonable and helpful for the others on the call.

Around the world, businesses are searching for ways to work leaner and smarter. Working virtually across countries, time zones, regions or counties is, in theory, a good way to stay connected and keep travel and accommodation costs down. Businesses must be competent at working virtually in order thrive and, meeting virtually (either with or without video) is today's reality.

The global economy is fragile and businesses are carefully watching the bottom line. There is an increase in virtual meetings – be they visual or audio.

Technology companies are getting better and better at supporting meaningful virtual meetings, and communication media is galloping ahead, with people actively staying connected through social media. Yet, at the same time, virtual business meetings are hitting a glass ceiling. I observe people depending on technology to make a success of their virtual meetings, if that sounds like you, I think you are looking in the wrong place. When you think about it, humans and their behaviour are at the heart of every meeting, virtual or not, and it is human behaviour that is struggling to keep up.

Do you recognize this? How can you break through?

I sometimes see eyes roll when virtual meetings are mentioned. When I ask "why", some people tell me that the biggest barriers are:

- That they feel nervous about the technology: "I don't know enough about technology to be comfortable."
- They expect to experience technical difficulty in both the meeting set-up and duration.
- I can't see people so it makes it hard to have a conversation.

A minority of my client organizations are focusing resources into building the physical, reliable hardware required to be able to work virtually. Even for them, with great technology in place, virtual meetings are still a bit clunky.

A project leader recently told me about his despair over a conference call he was "responsible for leading". His frustration was caused by two people on the call who were "at each other's throats, arguing, sparring and landing verbal blows".

The project leader shook his head. "How was I supposed to handle that?"

He told me how he had managed to progress the call but really wanted to "send them to their rooms to calm down".

I said it sounded as if the call could have benefited from having a facilitator, and he said "that's what I was supposed to be doing, but they were just so badly behaved, I wanted to stop the whole thing".

I felt for him because I recognized the situation only too well, and I hear these frustrations over and over again.

Our conversation went on and I asked what his biggest bugbear was. His reply came without hesitation: "technology: it's unreliable and so impersonal."

This project leader is not alone in his frustration, and joins the thousands of people who have mixed experiences of virtual meetings. Here was a competent man, with a great reputation for managing complex global projects, in despair about a virtual conversation and the behaviour that accompanied it.

My experience tells me that technology gets the blame, but it's attitudes that need fixing.

So, while it is true that technology plays a large and very important part in making virtual meetings work – even with the advances in technology, human beings are still required to make the most of the discussion structure, and it is human communication that is fast becoming the weakest link in the virtual chain. People are focusing more on the technology rather than on their attitude and behaviour.

I know clients who say "I've got a gem of an idea or a problem to solve, but getting everyone together from China, Australia and the US is too difficult – let's have a virtual meeting!" And that is when the fun begins.

Do this:
- **Begin with clarity of purpose.**
- **Be prepared to be fully present even though you can't be seen.**
- **Expect that some people will have stage fright. Many people still feel self-conscious in virtual meetings. They don't like not being able to see who they are speaking to. Then they become acutely aware of being heard virtually and it can impact their ability to communicate naturally.**
- **Expect real-time glitches with technology and be prepared to run with it and have a tech-savvy person on hand during those crucial meetings.**
- **Make the invisible, visible. Think about the engagement and stimulation required before, during and after a virtual meeting.**

- Expect side conversations to happen between virtual meeting participants. They happen naturally, and in a way, that is where the real conversation is taking place. You can include the value of these side conversations by acknowledging and encouraging them and agreeing a way to loop the highlights from them back into the main conversation.
- Have virtual coffee breaks: even virtual calls require occasional breaks – you should plan for them.

Stop this:
- Arranging virtual calls when you're travelling – it is not an efficient way to work for you or the others on the call.
- Thinking you can't be seen so I can behave as you like.
- Saying things you would never say in a face-to-face meeting, like saying "I'm going on mute", "sorry, I was multi-tasking, can you say that again?"

I am being purposefully provocative. I want to get you to think seriously about how you show up to virtual meetings and also about how you run them.

YOU CAN'T SEE ME!

KEEPING A RECORD

MEETING MINUTES

Do what is needed from the perspective of governance. But, don't create something that nobody remembers or recognizes.

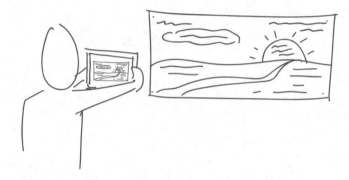

TOP TIP: You can make sure something really good happens after the meeting by thinking about how highlights of the discussions will be captured. Ask yourself: "what can I do to capture the content of this discussion so that it serves the group?"

The most useful minutes with which I work are photographs of the charts created in the meeting. If you take photographs of any notes produced in the meeting, you will have instant minutes that can be shared immediately.

Whichever way you minute a meeting, do it quickly while the meeting is fresh in everyone's minds

"Speech is conveniently located midway between thought and action, where it often substitutes for both"
John Andrew Holmes, poet and critic

This section focuses on the information being shared, exchanged, discussed in a meeting.

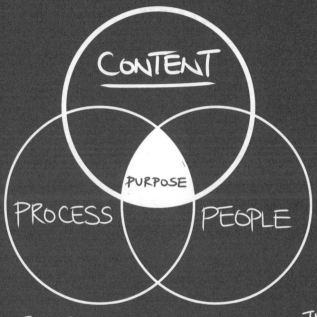

PART FIVE

THE TFP MEETING KALEIDOSCOPE ™

TWIST 4

CONTENT

THE CONTENT
OF A MEETING

"Companies and leaders who treat knowledge management as just another branch of IT don't understand how human beings learn and create"

Ikujiro Nonaka, Tokyo-based business scholar and
co-author of *The Knowledge Creating Company*

The content of a meeting is the information being shared and explored. Information tends to be present in meetings in the shape of:

· Data and facts
· Experience
· Opinions
· Feedback
· Insight

Too much information clogs up the system, slows down discussion and can leave some people behind.

Too little information results in a loss of insight, understanding and opportunity.

I often experience people in meetings put more effort into creating a PowerPoint presentation than into sharing, engaging, clarifying.

If you are intent on improving your meetings so that they achieve and deliver every time, you must get the balance just right. You need to look at the content of your meeting from a different angle – take time to consider a fresh perspective.

Think about content as an exchange of knowledge.

This view from Injuro Nonaka about knowledge shines this clarifying light:

"Knowledge is produced and consumed simultaneously. Its value increases with use, rather than being depleted as with industrial goods or commodities. Above all, it is a resource created by humans acting in relationship with one another."

The essence of the Meeting Kaleidoscope is to enable the purposeful sharing of the knowledge created by humans while acting in relationship with one another. Purpose, people, process and content.

For your next meeting, focus on what you want to achieve by establishing shared knowledge and understanding with the people there. Then work out how to share it to enable high-quality exchange.

THE QUEST FOR UNDERSTANDING

"Seek first to understand and then to be understood"

Stephen R Covey, educator and author

Even the sexiest PowerPoint deck will not achieve a shared exchange of content, no matter how well it is delivered. The reason is that sharing a deck is usually a one-way process. Presenter to listener.

Is it really the best use of those assembled brains to make them sit and watch a PowerPoint presentation? Are you really going to dim the lights and turn them into an 'audience'? If you treat the people in your meetings as an audience, guess what – that's how they'll behave. They will be passive observers who will rate you on your performance.

I'm being purposefully provocative. I do understand that sometimes it's best to share information with the group when they are all together, but far too many people use PowerPoint decks as a default way of running a meeting.

Content can be shared in many, many ways. The clarity, focus and ease with which content is shared will result in interpretation followed by understanding or misunderstanding. This is an important distinction. I say "understanding" but I don't say "agreement" or "disagreement". That's because the biggest key to exchanging and exploring information is simply to reach an understanding.

So much time is wasted in meetings because the emphasis is on persuasion, agreement and disagreement rather than reaching an understanding.

To understand is simply to understand – that's it. Only from a place of real understanding can you begin to form a view. The trouble is people tend to form their view before real understanding is reached and that is where misunderstanding and crossed-purposes come from. Misunderstanding is at the root of unhealthy meetings because so much is lost down the cracks of assumption.

Try this:

Step 1
Write a whole shopping list of all the content you want to add to a meeting.

Step 2
Look at the list and ask yourself:

- What understanding is needed in this meeting to move us towards our purpose and goals?
- What information do the brains in this meeting need to understand together so that they can consider, discuss, share, debate, work out, solve?
- What background or contextual information do we need to understand in order to move our thinking on?

The answers to these questions will help you to work out what information, knowledge, content is required in order that people have what they need to fully understand.

Separate out what you think you should discuss and what you really need to discuss. Then edit your list.

WELCOME A NAIVE POINT OF VIEW

Do you need to understand the subject matter to spark, or contribute to, a great conversation?

A good friend of mine was recently in a meeting and boldly asked "does anybody here actually know what a hashtag is?" As she said it a few people laughed and others breathed a sigh of relief that she had asked the very question they felt unable to.

It reminds me of the story of *The Emperor's New Clothes* by Hans Christian Anderson about two weavers who promise an emperor a beautiful new suit that is invisible to those who are stupid or incompetent. When the emperor parades before his subjects in his new suit, nobody dares to say they cannot see it until a child cries out, "but he isn't wearing anything at all!"

A number of morals can be found in that tale, yet my focus is on the naivety of the child in the crowd who shouts out that the emperor is naked. The child speaks the truth, because children tend not to be bound by the rules of politics or peer pressure.

If you are smart, you will invite somebody to your meetings who has a similar naivety – perhaps somebody without any vested interest in the subject being discussed. Their brief should be to be curious and to point out what they see.

It's a good move to have a way of asking the (apparently) "dumb" question in meetings, because everyone assumes that everyone else understands everything, and that they are the only one who doesn't. Not knowing or being scared to ask is not a good foundation for creating shared understanding.

Here are a handful of questions that, when asked with genuine curiosity, could help you:

- How can we be certain?
- What do we know for sure?
- Why is this important now?
- What could be possible?
- What might we be missing?

A BRIEF WORD ABOUT THE CHRISTMAS PARTY AGENDA ITEM

This is the subject guaranteed to get everyone fired up and can be the most hotly debated item on the agenda. The one that gets even the quietest person in the room to contribute.

Where to have it?
Should it be themed? Fancy dress?
(that story about Jeremy from accounts last year - giggle)
Will the organization pay?
When shall we have it?

It's almost as if the meeting only really comes freely alive at this point.

Why? Because people care about it and have opinions they want to share.

How can you make the content of your meeting as engaging and spark as much passion as the subject of the Christmas party?

- **Be crystal clear about why the meeting has been called.**
- **Be clear and aligned about what needs to be achieved by the end of the meeting.**
- **Invite the right people for the conversations to be had.**
- **Help them to understand why their contribution is needed.**
- **Be choosy about each and every agenda item.**
- **Create space and time in the agenda to do each item justice.**
- **Agree with the group how decisions will be made.**
- **Make sure the group are part of the outcome of the meeting.**

PREPARATION
AND PRE-READS

INVITE PEOPLE TO PARTICIPATE, NOT TO BE AN AUDIENCE

If you really do want your meetings to deliver and achieve every time, you will stop taking up valuable minutes (sometimes hours) sharing information that could have been shared ahead of time.

Preparing people in advance of a meeting helps to create more value during the meeting itself. By sharing some information before you hold the meeting, along with a question about that information, allows people to reflect ahead of time to be more resourceful when they are together. They will arrive more prepared and ready to engage.

It makes sense that preparing people in advance of a meeting helps to create more value during the meeting itself. But how can you engage people beforehand to make sure that time spent in the meeting is productive and gets the best out of everybody attending?

You may already send out 'pre-reads' with the intention of sharing important information before the meeting, to help deepen the discussion during it. This intention is spot on, but often the reality is overwhelming – especially if there is a pre-read for each agenda item.

BE SMART WITH PRE-READS – LESS IS MORE

You might be turning people off before meetings with extensive pre-reading. Be choosy about what needs to be seen or read ahead of time.

Focus the pre-read with a question, for example:

- · What opportunities do you see here?
- · What challenges do you see that we must pay attention to?

BEFORE, DURING, AFTER

Think of the meeting as part of an ongoing discussion – it's the bit where people come together for discussion.

Remember, if the sole focus of your meetings is to achieve a shared understanding of the information, opinion, facts, insights, data and inspiration, you would take a big step forward by having meetings that achieve and deliver every time.

*"If we all did the things we are capable of,
we would literally astound ourselves"*
Thomas A Edison, inventor and businessman

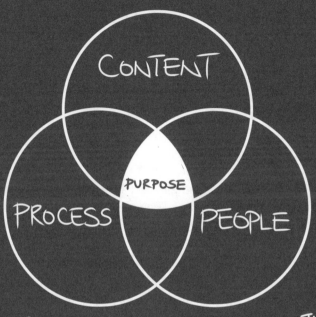

PART SIX

THE TFP MEETING KALEIDOSCOPE ™

MAKING IT
HAPPEN

FOCUS ON
MEETING CULTURE

"Everything is energy and that's all there is to it. Match the frequency of the reality you want and you cannot help but to get the reality. It can be no other way. This is not philosophy. This is physics"

Einstein

The tone, feel, rhythm, tempo and effectiveness of your meetings (and the meetings all around you) contribute to the overall culture of your organization. Every move you make counts towards this being a great place to work – or not.

It is true that the culture of your organization is the combination of many things, including what you produce, the personalities of senior leaders, the influence of customers and stakeholders – I could go on. All of these things blend to create the overall feel. Each element creates an energy that bounces around to create an atmosphere.

Meetings play an enormous part in that.

As you read this, the people of the world are taking part in a collective energy; a rhythm of travelling to meetings, contributing, moving on...and so it perpetuates.

Look around you: that guy in the car as he drives by; the man on the train who keeps losing his signal; that girl as she dials into a conference call; that boss with a closed door in a one-to-one discussion. All of them in meeting after meeting after meeting.

Now, study this picture more closely: you will notice that meeting culture is conducted by the 'few' and attended by the 'many'. The few are well-intentioned and the many go along with it. The few send out an agenda, a list of important subjects to be shared, 'discussed', or outlined. The many sit through, hour after hour, waiting for the part of the agenda to which they can contribute, only to find that time has run out and that point will be added to next week's agenda. The few arrange their next meeting and the many attend their next meeting. And the cycle repeats itself.

That is hard to change – who wants to stick their head above the parapet? Who dares to speak up and say "I know a better way?"

There are people inside most organizations whose meeting styles do not align perfectly with the culture of the business. It turns out that their ways of working are different and that includes their approach to meetings.

It is a mistake to assume that it's the creative departments, such as marketing, in which all the creative meetings happen. On the contrary, I know many a finance team that have great meetings. But these are often the exceptions, and the exceptions are driven by the beliefs, tone and tempo of an individual who doesn't quite fit the organization's cultural norm.

I'm not in every meeting room, and there are always exceptions to every pattern; however, I've attended enough meetings over the past 30 years to be confident of making some generalizations.

What do you recognize?

Do you have sufficient dissatisfaction to want to make your meetings better?

There are several places where meetings work very well. Places in which each individual looks forward to meetings because they know why their contribution is needed.

These are where there is a variety of:

- Fast-paced, spontaneous, "pop-up" meetings, aimed at quick alignment and decision-making.
- Longer, "planned for" meetings aimed at developing strategy, reviewing progress, solving sticky problems, creating new possibilities.

Whatever the purpose of your meeting, the way you approach it will create a culture in it and around it. This is what you will be known for and that will have a direct impact on the overall culture of your organization. Be aware of:

- The behaviour you demonstrate.
- How sharp and intentional your approach is.
- How you make decisions.
- How you prepare "fertile ground" for the meeting.
- The speed, style, pace and tone.
- The way you "get at" the issues you face rather than simply "getting around" them.

All of these things influence your meeting culture for the long term.

If you have ever attended a training course about how to have successful meetings, and left that course feeling energized and clear about the changes you want to make to the way you run your meetings, you will – I'm certain of it – have faced an up-hill battle to turn that intention into reality. You are among the few if you survived unscathed. Why? Because an organization's meeting culture begins with the culture of the organization itself – it is not confined to, or isolated within, a meeting room. The tone and tempo of your organization's meetings begin with the tone and tempo of the people that your organization employs. And that begins at the top. It is a simple cause-and-effect equation.

THE GAP BETWEEN KNOWING AND DOING

"People are always blaming circumstances for what they are; I don't believe in circumstances. The people who get ahead in this world are the people who get up and look for the circumstances they want, and if they can't find them, make them"

George Bernard Shaw, playwright

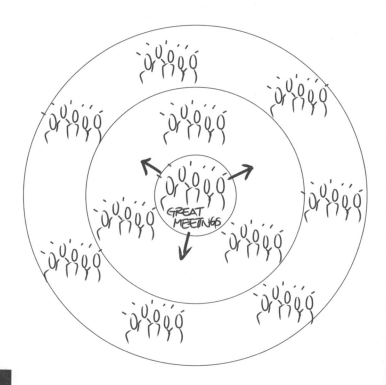

There exists a gap. It's a gap between what you know about good meetings and what you do about it.

As I said at the outset, nothing will change just because you read a book. To make a change, you have to do something. That will take energy, intention, commitment and a willingness to learn.

The truth is that the meetings you call and the meetings you attend can change rapidly and positively as a result of you. You are the fulcrum, the point of balance. You have a place in the system, whether you are the meeting 'owner', 'leader', 'facilitator', 'chairperson' or an 'ordinary participant'. How you show up; your attitude; your expectations; your focus, has an impact on the entire system. So, decide to do something with what you know:

- Use the lens of the Meeting Kaleidoscope to see what is going on: purpose, people, process and content.
- Deal with meetings' qualities, not with their quantities – make the moves you need to make to gain:

1. Crystal clarity of purpose.
2. The right people who know why their contribution is needed.
3. A good process to enable a good conversation.
4. The right content (knowledge, information, data, fact, opinion) to be shared and decided upon.

- Focus on your goal and be prepared to adapt and communicate during your meetings to achieve it (rather than forcing yourself and your group through a rigid agenda).
- Bring intention and intensity to your meetings and leave ego outside the door.

TOP-DOWN

Take a big step back, look at the culture of your business, along with its meeting routines and framework, and make the change from that point – the top-down approach. The top-down approach may need to begin and be role-modelled by the most senior people in your organization.

You can influence that, all you need is the first conversation.

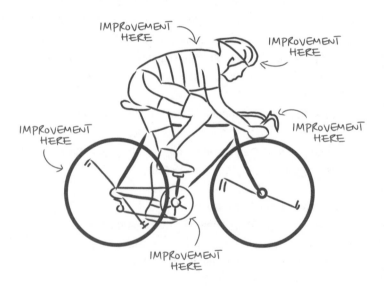

1% MARGIN IMPROVEMENT

Even small changes to your meeting routines will result in substantial improvement over time. In his time at UK Cycling, Sir Dave

Brailsford decided on a simple approach; he believed in a concept that he referred to as the "aggregation of marginal gains". He talked about his ambition to achieve a "1% margin for improvement in everything you do".

You can do that. Simply begin with your next meeting and keep going, bit by bit, move by move.

THE BUTTERFLY'S FLUTTER

It has been said that something as small as the flutter of a butterfly's wing can ultimately cause a typhoon halfway around the world. Change one thing, change everything. Just like all new things, one purposeful act can begin a ripple that begins a positive shift for many. This is the butterfly effect.

BE THE PERSON WHO GOES FIRST

There is some comfort in knowing that your current meeting routine is safe.

Nothing will change just because you read a book.

To make a change you need to be brave.

Have clear purpose, be your best self to serve the best in others, be creative with process, think about content as knowledge.

Over to you now.

REFERENCES

Simon Sinek, *Start with Why* (Penguin, 2011)

Richard Olivier, *Inspirational Leadership* (Spiro Press, 2003)

Robert T Kiyosaki, *Rich Dad, Poor Dad* (Plata Publishing, 2011)

Steven Pressfield, *Turning Pro: Tap Your Inner Power and Create Your Life's Work* (Black Irish Entertainment LLC, 2012)

Sam Kaner, *The Facilitator's Participatory Decision Making* (Jossey-Bass, 2014)

Hans Christian Anderson, *The Emperor's New Clothes* (C.A. Reitzel, 1837)

Ikujiro Nonaka and Hirotaka Takeuchi, *The Knowledge Creating Company* (Oxford University Press, 1995)

David Sibbett, *Visual Meetings: How Graphics, Sticky Notes and Idea Mapping Can Transform Group Productivity* (Wiley, 2011)

ABOUT THE AUTHOR

Helen Chapman is a director and founding partner of The Facilitation Partnership and Inky Thinking.

She is a business leader and professional facilitator with 25 years' experience supporting leaders and teams in global FMCGs, consumer electronics, aviation, energy supply and construction. Helen holds an MBA from Oxford Brookes University and is a practitioner of both the Myers-Briggs Type indicator (MBTi) and Neuro-Linguistic Programming (NLP).

Helen lives in the UK and is mother to three artistic and musical children.

Contact the author for: facilitation, facilitation training or meeting consultation.

helen@thefacilitationpartnership.com
+44 2031 433 433
www.thefacilitationpartnership.com
www.inkythinking.com